Little Miracles

Jason Morgan

BookLeaf Publishing

India | USA | UK

Presentation by *BookLeaf Publishing*

Web: www.bookleafpub.com

E-mail: info@bookleafpub.com

ISBN: 9789358319774

First edition 2023

DEDICATION

To my wife, Andrea, who's consistent and unwavering support is summed up as "Go for it babe, sounds like fun."

ACKNOWLEDGEMENT

I want to thank Bookleaf Publishing for the opportunity afforded me to put my creativity out into the world.

Sparky

Wet kisses and playful bites
Running and playing into the nights
Bye Sparky, you were the best
The goodest of boys, better than the rest
There'll never be another as good as you
Friends like us, there are few
Always loyal and always there
I'm not sure where to go from here
It's been a while but you're still missed
Mum's putting me in an arm-twist
To see if I will want a new best friend
But my love for you isn't at an end
I look at this pretender, this imposter
Tolerating his smile is taking all I can muster
He jumps around trying to play
I should just tell him to go away!
He took a tumble playing with the hose
I guess he looks cute…I suppose
Now he's snuggling into me under my arm
Maybe he can stay for a while, what's the harm?
You'll never be Sparky, but…you do seem ok
We can go for a walk, but just for today
You'll probably go back tomorrow, or maybe the
next day
Hey, wait for me! Don't forget I want to play!

Connect

Faces in phones,
Humpbacked bodies
No talking just groans
All carbon copies
Surrounded and alone
Suffocated by separation
Remain within your zone
Conversation is an aberration
There's a pause in the air
Feeling eyes rest on you
Not knowing from where
Slowly look up taking the cue
A head not looking down
Eyes meet eyes with purpose
Face a coffee brown
A respite in this dark circus
Lips stretched wide
Reveal a hint of teeth
A smile provides light
I feel myself breathe
Relaxed and warm
A gesture so tiny
Yet the gloom is torn
Just enough to free me
And to wrap me in it

Giving energy to my stride
Helping me to not quit
The dark is for now, denied

Another Dollar

Beep!
Uh..ugh
What Da fug?
What is the time?
Gotta change that chime.
Work should be made a crime.
Better get myself up now.
Dressed. Breakfast, And a hot shower.
Drag myself out of the house.
Feel the sun on me now.
Close my eyes and smile.
Think maybe I'll
Even smile
Today

Go Get It

5

Pretty packaging
Crinkly and bright
Extra sweet, extra salty
Turn down the light

I don't want to see
The mess of the feast
It all looks too much
I must be a beast

Listless and sad
I check on the scales
To see what I know
Another day of fails

The mirror the same
No help to be found
I turn away from myself
I sink to the ground

Small change is needed
Large was too much
A little less junk food
Perhaps just a touch

More water not fizz
These things aren't too hard
Less TV at night
And night snacks are barred

It's been four months now
And my energy is better
I sleep better too
And walk in all weather

It didn't take a lot
But I had to stick at it
Once the habits are there
I started to get fit

Happier now
Looking forward to more
Enjoying good food
Is no longer a chore

Reveal

White space
Staring back at me
Reflecting emptiness

Suffocated by options
Brush weighs heavy
Wet with potential

Paint meets canvas
Violated with colour
Forced across the surface

Bright and formless
Unfolding before me
I witness the reveal

My arm is the tool
The brush is the artist
The paint, inspiration

I recognise, I understand
I am now given control
Worthy to direct

The image reaches out to me
Trusting me on the final path
To guide it forth

We see each other

The Rush

9

I have bet it all
The high of the win so strong
The loss so crushing

Please

Yearning.
Overwhelmed.
Unfathomable.

Why?
Is this the end?
Love is forever.
Liar.

Broken.
Embarrassed.

Owe me an explanation.
Kiss me, please.

Tears.
How?
I don't understand.
Stay.

Tell me what I need to do?
Only you.
Only me?

Stop.

Hold me.
Anger.
Leave me alone!
Lament.

Pain.
Adjust.
Silence.
Still.

Dad

Why did you die?
Why aren't you here?
I'm scared all the time,
But you're not there
Not there to smile
And make me brave
Not there at all
Just make-believe
I share my secrets
But there's no reply
No arms to hold me
When I cry
I'm lonely and small
But the oldest of all
I have to be the grown up now
But I'm too small, I don't know how
Mum needs me to help
But it isn't fair
Can't I just be a kid?
Why aren't you here?
I'm finishing school now
I'll have a job soon enough
I'm not mad anymore
But I still find it tough
I wish you were able to tell me

You're proud of who I am
I wish you could see me now
Tell me I'm becoming a man
I've traveled the world now
I have a home of my own
With my wife and children
My eldest is all grown
I sometimes have moments
Where I'm quiet and sad
Moments when I wonder
What life would've been with you Dad
Then I stare at these young faces
And you look back at me smiling
You're no longer gone
But I still feel like crying
They're happy tears now
Not realising back then
That I'd look at my children and see you in
them.

Umm...Whoops?

Where the hell are they?
You know what I mean!
They are always here.
Where could they have been?

So what if they're cheap?
I have to find them now!
I need to wear them tonight..
Stop being such a cow!

You've always been jealous
They look so good on me
You wish you had my style
And everyone can see

You trying to copy my look
I bet that you stole them
I can't believe your gall
I'm so mad I…oh, ahem..

Haha you won't believe this
My beautiful best friend
They might have been in my pocket…
Good news for us in the end?

Hehe so funny how I was joking
What a funny sight
Me pretending I had lost them
Haha..ha..ha..right?

Is There More?

Spring in my step I need to restore
Late nights staying up the day before

Would love to leave it
But have to stay put

Buying lotto tickets at the store
Wanting to call in sick a lot more

Bills are there to pay
So I have to stay

But how to keep chin up
Always booze in my cup

What did I want to be
When did it leave me

Energy low when the workday completed
A to do list of interests always repeated

Earlier nights, quieten the noise
Less booze, better food, healthier choice

Block out some time for fun
Exercise and getting things done

Some things are free that I love to do
With my family or even alone too

A small block for my clarity
Just for what helps my sanity

This will be a help when the office spins
And the walls feel big and try to close in

Knowing this isn't all I am or 1 do
Is what gives me the strength to get through

Each day and each week something for me
To help keep me going, to help me be free.

Recover in Green

Breathe in.
Smell of the wild.
The green, swaying leaves.

Warm sun.
Cool of the trees.
Soft dirt underneath.

No cars.
No timetables.
City sounds are all gone.

Eyes close.
Let stillness in.
Feel the calm take over.

Reset.
This is the place.
Refresh and repeat.

Moment in Time

The other side of me
Closer than blood
We are no longer we
Reduced to "Bud"

When did this happen?
Was it recent?
Or long term action?
It seems silent.

No conversation had
To explain or decide
No one feeling bad
Neither one to deride.

Have I changed or have you?
Did we just grow apart?
Do you feel like this too?
I still care in my heart.

But the bond isn't there
Like it was for so long
It's ok you're not here
No one did any wrong

I wish you the best and
I hope you will find
The right fit for your plans
What you have in mind

We will find happiness
But not together
All our good times I'll miss
They weren't forever

I know that without those
We couldn't become
Once joined but now solos
Yet a good outcome

Free to be who we are
Both happy and whole
Much more grown than we were
Our heart and our soul.

Gym

Eyes.
Thighs.
My thighs.
Their eyes.
Why?

Sweat.
Regret.
Go home.
You gnome.
Alone.

"Hi."
"Hi."
"Welcome."
"Have fun."
"C'mon."

Change

Yearn for more.
I know the score.
Need to change.
Increase my range.

Stuck in a rut.
Old habits to cut.
New me starts now.
This is my vow.

Refine the rough.
Goodbye old stuff
that didn't work.
Goodbye to that jerk.

More enlightened
Don't be frightened.
I'll still be here
Just much more clear

On what to keep
And what to sweep
I don't want to
Start to lose who

I like in me
While getting free
Of the habits
That are bad fits

For who I should
Be now for good.
This is the start
Follow my heart

Old me not lost
Good parts not tossed
But added into
The me that's true.

New Start

Outgrew
All of you
Change was needed
So that's what I did

Settled
New house filled
New memories
Friends, job and hobbies

Not sad
I'm so glad
I was strong
Didn't stay too long

And now
I see how
The best is yet
There for me to get

P.B.

Oh my god
I did it at last
Finally

Been so long
After all my work
Goal is reached

Can I relax?
It is now flipped.
Was the goal

Now the base
It's where I start now
To go on

It was once
My inspiration
Now it is

My old low
Always chasing more
I love it

Treasure Chest

Grudgingly going to work
Feeling low
Work sucks
Hard
Others the same
Boss is rubbish
Treats me bad
Sweating and tired
Ache everywhere
Finally sit down
What is the point?
Note in my lunchbox
Written in crayon
"You're the greatest, Dad."

I am Enough

Lonely or just alone?
I'm ok on my own.
No sadness or longing
I don't feel it's boring

Happy around others
Had my share of lovers
But don't feel I'm hearing
A half of me calling

I have great connections
With friends like I've mentioned
But I'm just as happy
Hanging out with just me

Some moments are nicer
And the choice is wiser
To avoid forced events
Even though they're with friends

And to opt for solace
Not meaning no malice
To those that invite us
I don't want any fuss

When I want to, I'll come
And if not, I'll be home
And either way suits me
As long as I feel free

It's a good way to live
And I'm happy to give
My time when I choose it
So simple isn't it?

When The World Stood Still

What's happening to the world?
New rules everyday.
This madness has unfurled.
Nothing good to say.

Every cough there's danger.
Masks cover up the face.
Stay away from strangers.
End of human race?

Travelling has ended.
Lockdowns are in force.
People that depended
On others are hit worst

Less traffic on the road
Staying home from work.
Being forced into slow mode
Almost like a perk.

We're not all in a rush
Have time for a breath
Natural land is lush
Still a tragic mess

People are connecting
Less air pollution
Perhaps this direction
Stops the illusion

That everything was fine
Before we were sick
This is your world and mine
Stop being so thick

Let's all work together
Saw a glimpse of change
If we just surrender
Our selfish exchange

The Leap

Is it too soon?
Why does he swoon?

I'm not healed yet
The hurt is set.

How could I try?
I should say "Bye"

But it might be
The one for me

Shouldn't I be
Also happy?

Hurt once before
To love no more

That's not living
He's so giving

Why rob myself
Of love itself?

I'll take the plunge

Of life's challenge

To risk the hurt
Sure to assert

The love I make
No one's to take

But mine to give
Best way to live

Little Miracles

My bodyguard
Is the world around
And all the tiny things
I see each day

They remind me
Of the miracles
Of which, I am one of
That gives me pause

To reflect on
How we all connect
And how joy can be found
If you let it

The taste of food
The laugh of a friend
The smile of a stranger
Warmth of a bath

Sound of the sea
The sun on your face
Or dancing and singing
People watching

Reading a book
Painting a picture
Watching the wind in trees
And so much more

They are what helps
When the world seems big
Like a dark tidal wave
Small is ok

Solace is small
Small can be wonder
Small can help you recharge
And can give strength

So the big waves
Don't crash on me
But instead let me ride
With them in peace.

9 789358 319774